dealing with RELATIONSHIPS

Marcella Forster

Wayland

Bullying
Eating Disorders
Relationships
Substance Abuse
Death
Family Break-up

Book editor: Louise Woods
Series editor: Deb Elliott
Concept design: Joyce Chester
Book design: Helen White

First published in 1995 by Wayland (Publishers) Ltd
61 Western Road, Hove,
East Sussex BN3 1JD

British Library Cataloguing in Publication Data
Forster, Marcella
Relationships. - (Dealing With Series)
I. Title II. Series
305.235

ISBN 0 7502 0993 3

Typeset by White Design
Printed and bound by Canale in Italy

All of the people who appear in the photographs in this book are models.

Acknowledgements
The publishers would like to thank the following for allowing their photographs to be reproduced in this book:
Eye Ubiquitous: 5 and 10 (Skjold), 8, 29 and 30 (Paul Seheult), 31 (Dave Fobister), 39 (Mostyn 92); Lupe Cunha: 42; Photri Inc: 13; Sally and Richard Greenhill: 6 (Sally Greenhill), 7, 15, 20 (Richard Greenhill), 44 top, 45; Timothy Woodcock Photo Library: 12, 26, 28, 32, 34, 36, 37, 38; Tony Stone Worldwide: 33 (Don Smetzer); Wayland Picture Library: 11, 16, 17, 19, 21, 22, 23, 24, 40, 41, 43 (all Andrew Perris), 18 (WPL).

Contents

Parents

▶ **Ignoring your parents' rules will often make them try and keep even more control over you.**

Do you and your parents seem to row about everything? About how you dress and have your hair, how loud you have your music, what to watch on television, how late you can stay out or the kind of friends you have? If so, you are not alone. Though these arguments seem to be about all kinds of things, in fact most of them are really about control, about who is in charge of your life: you or your parents.

From the moment you emerge into this world as a baby, you struggle for independence from your parents. Gradually you learn to do things for yourself. Soon you can walk, talk and feed yourself. Adolescence is the final step along the road to taking control of your own life. It would be wonderful if parents gradually handed over responsibility to their teenagers at a rate that satisfied both sides. However, for a number of reasons, things are not usually that easy.

'They treat me like a child.'

Parents are often not sure whether to treat their teenager as a child or as an adult, especially if this is their first child. Some cultures have a ceremony that marks a child's passage to adulthood, so everyone knows when that person should be given adult privileges and responsibilities. But in most Western cultures there is no clear point when someone becomes an adult. Even the law is confusing in this respect. While you can get married at sixteen, you cannot legally drive until you are seventeen or vote until you are eighteen.

Generally, teenagers want more freedom than their parents feel comfortable about. So the relationship can feel like a tug of war, with teenagers striving for more independence, and parents holding them back. Parents tend

Laura Huddlestone opened the front door and tiptoed inside, carefully avoiding making any noise. She smiled to herself as she remembered Rob's kiss. What a night! And he had asked her to go out with him again tomorrow.

'What time do you call this, madam?'

Laura nearly jumped out of her skin. Her mum was sitting at the table in the kitchen, looking furious.

'Sorry I'm a bit late, Mum.'

'A bit late? It's past midnight, child.'

'Don't call me 'child'. I'm fourteen.'

'You *are* a child. You can't even stick to a simple rule, can you? Eleven o'clock is what I said, and eleven o'clock is what I meant.' Mrs. Huddlestone was seething.

'All my friends are allowed to stay out till midnight on Fridays.'

'I don't care about anyone else.'

'You can say that again,' Laura muttered.

'Right, I've had it with you! You're not leaving this house till Monday morning when you go to school.'

'Mum! You can't do that!'

'I just have.' Mrs Huddlestone marched upstairs towards her bedroom.

'You can't make me stop in,' Laura shouted.

'I'll just run away.'

Laura's mum spun around. Her eyes were filled with anger.

'And don't think you're using the phone to ring loverboy. You're banned from that as well.'

'I hate you!' Laura screamed. 'I hate you!' She ran up to her bedroom and slammed the door.

to be cautious because they worry that their teenagers are not yet mature enough to cope with the temptations of the adult world, such as sex, drugs and crime. If anything goes wrong, they feel responsible.

A further complication is that teenagers often have mixed feelings about becoming adult. While they naturally strive to become independent of their parents, they are sometimes frightened at the prospect of leaving home and managing alone. Consequently they may find themselves demanding the right to stay out all night one minute and wanting to be pampered and given a mug of cocoa in bed the next. They swing from behaving like an adult to behaving like a child.

Parents' feelings

Meanwhile, parents, too, feel ambivalent about their children becoming adults. Though some look forward to the extra time and money they will have when their children leave home, others – especially those whose main occupation has been looking after

their children – may feel there will no longer be any point to their lives. In addition, seeing their children nearing adulthood is a reminder for parents that their own youth is over and that they may never realize the dreams they once had. This confusion of feelings can lead parents to treat their teenagers like children, while expecting them to behave like adults.

Showing your parents that you are ready for responsibility will also help them to view you as an adult. It sounds boring, but if you take on jobs like washing up without having to be forced to do so (no one expects you to *like* these jobs!), then your parents are likely to think you are ready for more independence.

As children, our emotional ties to our parents are very strong. These ties have to be loosened when we are teenagers so that we can feel free to build close emotional bonds outside the family, particularly in romantic relationships.

▲ Many parents dread their children leaving home. They think their lives will have no point any more.

▶ If your parents come from a different country, you may live in one culture at home and in another one with your friends.

Single parents

Making the emotional break from a single parent may be particularly hard, especially if you are an only child. Your parent may be frightened at the prospect of you growing up and leaving them alone. Sometimes they might resort to emotional blackmail, asking you to stay in at night instead of going out with your friends, because they don't want to feel lonely. Don't feel you have to succumb to this pressure. Instead, they should be building a social life for themselves.

> Jamilla's parents moved from India to England before she was born. She has never been to India. Jamilla wants to do the same things as her friends: go to parties, hang around the shopping precinct, go out with boys. But her parents have different ideas. They have arranged for her to marry their friends' son from India, so they won't let her go out with boys. Jamilla is furious. She says it is her life and she will do what she wants. If she ever marries, it will be to someone she is in love with.

Immigrant parents

If your parents moved to the United Kingdom from another country with a different culture, you may face challenges resulting from a clash of cultures.

Preserving the culture of their native country is understandably important to many immigrants. Jamilla lived an Indian way of life at home and a British life at school and with her friends. When her parents insisted on an arranged marriage, she felt she had to choose between the two cultures. Meanwhile, her parents could not understand her objection to an arranged marriage: their own love for each other had grown *after* their marriage which, in turn, had been arranged by their parents.

If you are in a situation like this, it is important to pursue your own desires, even if this upsets your parents. You may need the help of a sympathetic adult from within your parents' community to help you explain this to them. Try not to attack your parents' beliefs – everyone is entitled to their own ideas.

Running away

Most young people think about running away from home at some point. They might think of doing this to punish their parents or they might be unable to cope with what is going on at home, especially if they are being abused.

Running away is a serious matter. You might have enough money to last for a while, but it will soon run out. Getting a job that pays

◀ **Running away probably will not solve your problems. Getting some help might.**

enough for somewhere to live, bills and food is very difficult. This is one reason why so many young people who do run away from home find themselves homeless and forced into prostitution or other criminal activities. Most of them certainly did not plan things that way. But there are always unscrupulous adults on the lookout for runaways whom they can exploit.

If things are so bad at home that you feel you must escape, there are other options than running away and endangering yourself. Maybe you could move in with a grandparent or a friend, for example. If you are sixteen or over, it is possible to have yourself placed in the care of Social Services. If you are under sixteen, they can help you negotiate with your parents. For more information on this, call your local Social Services office. Remember, your aim in escaping the home situation is to make things better for yourself. Running away to a strange city and fending for yourself will not achieve this.

Dealing with conflict

What is the best way of dealing with the differences between what you and your parents want? Everybody has their own style of dealing with conflict. Some parents are determined to get their own way. They make the rules, then tell their children, 'You'll do it because I say so.' They may even use physical force to control their children. As their children get older and bigger, parents will find it more and more difficult to force them to do as they are told. This method of problem-solving is not successful with teenagers.

Other parents always let their teenagers have their own way. They may resist to begin with, but if their teenager has a tantrum or blackmails them, they give in. You may think it would be great to have parents who let you do whatever you wanted. However, if parents don't set guidelines, teenagers usually feel unsure of whether their parents love them. Teenagers who get away with blackmailing their parents become miserable, self-centred and do not respect others' needs. They may have difficulty in making friends because they think their needs are always more important than everybody else's.

If you and your parents are locked into one of the above styles of dealing with conflict, you might try a different method. Suggest sitting down together and listening carefully, without interruption, as each person explains what they are worried about and what they want. Then work towards a solution that suits everyone. This takes time, but it does leave everybody feeling that what they want is important and respected and that they have contributed towards the solution. Everyone then feels motivated to stick to the deal.

Getting through it

It may seem as if the teenager-parent relationship is a nightmare, full of resentment, pain and arguments. But there are positive aspects. Some parents and teenagers share an interest in clothes, music or sports, and many parents love having a houseful of their teenager's friends.

If fierce arguments are making you feel as if your relationship with your parents has completely broken down, remember that this state of affairs will not last forever. It is a normal part of growing up. Though it might be hard to imagine at the moment, you and your parents may be able to look back and laugh about it one day.

▼ Try to resolve conflicts by family discussion instead of by argument.

Family break-up and divorce

▲ It can come as a terrible shock to children when a family breaks up.

Every day about 500 children and young people in the UK discover that their parents have decided to live apart. Though divorce or separation is a horribly painful experience for everyone involved, it is especially difficult for young people. For some, it will be the worst thing that has ever happened to them.

Thirteen-year-old Alison knew her parents argued a lot. One morning she got up and found her mum crying. Alison's mum told her that her dad had left them and wasn't coming back. Alison couldn't believe it. When she asked her mum why, she said it was because they argued. This did not seem like much of a reason to Alison. Everyone's parents argued.

Though there is no way to avoid the misery that separation and divorce bring, there are things that can help you get through this difficult time.

The break-up

Some young people are not surprised when their family breaks up, but for others, divorce or separation comes as a terrible shock.

Most parents do not explain well to their children why they are splitting up. In fact, Alison's dad had fallen in love with someone else, but her mum was too embarrassed to tell her.

Generally, young people are better able to cope with divorce if they are given the information they want. The questions most people want their parents to answer are: Why are you splitting up? Are you separating for ever or just for a while? Are you getting divorced? Where am I going to live? Will I still see my mum/dad?

If you are in a family that is going through a separation or divorce and you feel confused, ask your parents to tell you what their plans are. Although they may not be able to tell you immediately, if they keep you informed of what is going on, it will help you feel less frightened.

How your parents feel

Just when you most need your parents to help you, they may be unable to give you the support you need. Alison's mum was ashamed that her husband loved someone else instead of her. She was so overwhelmed by what had happened that she didn't have any energy left over to think about Alison's needs. She took no interest in anything and stopped doing the shopping.

Alison was upset by her mum's behaviour. Alison needed to feel loved and reassured that everything was going to be all right. Instead, she was having to look after her mum.

▶ **Parents, too, are often overwhelmed by a divorce.**

▼ **Always ask your parents to explain what is going to happen.**

If you are in this kind of situation, don't feel you have to cope on your own. Make sure that you have someone you can talk to about your feelings, maybe a close friend or a relative. Alison finally phoned her aunt, who came to help out for a week. This gave both Alison and her mum someone to talk to.

'Who should I live with?'
When parents separate, a decision has to be made about where the children will live. You should have a say in this decision if you want to. Some parents do not think to ask their children for their opinions, so it is important to tell your parents what you want.

Choosing who to live with is not choosing who you love most. Whoever you are with, you are bound to miss the other parent and they will miss you. It is important to live where you will be happiest, and this might mean staying near your friends and at the same school.

All kinds of living arrangements are possible. Some children whose parents live close to each other spend half the week with one parent and half with the other. It can be confusing having two homes, but it works out for some people. Discuss the possibilities with your parents.

◀ You may find you have to help out more at home.

Practical changes
There are usually some practical adjustments to make following a separation or divorce. You may have to move house or even move to a different part of the country. Moving a long way off can make things very difficult for young people because it may rob them of the friends they can confide in and be with.

Money worries are another strain that divorce usually brings. Often there is less money available than before, so the parent who lives with the children may have to work longer hours. Children and teenagers may find themselves having to help out a lot at home or even being put under pressure to leave school and get a job sooner than they want.

Keeping in touch
When a parent moves out, children go through the same kinds of feelings as they would if that parent had died. Not surprisingly, many people feel angry with their parents for putting them through so much pain and confusion. However, when a family breaks up it is important for children to keep in touch with the parent they no longer live with. At first this may be difficult. You will probably feel abandoned by the

parent who left. It may seem that you can avoid your feelings by not seeing that parent. But these feelings will keep coming back if you don't see that parent and deal with the problem. Telling your parent how you feel will help.

There can be practical difficulties in seeing your parent if they move a long way off. You may only be able to see them during school holidays. It will probably be strange seeing them in unfamiliar surroundings to begin with, and you may wonder what you are going to talk about. You might have to cope with their new relationship, if they have one, which will present a new set of problems. Though these difficulties are all hard to deal with, they are not as awful as the grief and loss you will feel if you never see your parent again. It is worth knowing that, in nearly all cases, children of divorced parents do better emotionally in the long term if they keep in touch with both their parents.

If your absent parent is not good at keeping in touch, it is not because they do not love you. It may be because they feel guilty for causing you pain and think that they will do less harm if they stay out of your life. They might also feel embarrassed about having a new partner. If you can, tell them how important it is for you to continue seeing each other.

Adjusting

It takes a long time for a family to settle down after a separation or divorce. It may take a year or more to adjust to the practical changes and even longer to settle down emotionally. If you feel up to it, try to get involved in the decisions that affect you. This will help you feel less frightened and more in control of what is happening in your life. When you are overwhelmed by problems and confusion, try to talk to someone outside the family – a friend, a teacher or a relative. If you have no one you can talk to, phone one of the organizations listed in the back of this book. They are there to help you and give you support.

◀ It may be difficult to deal with your parent's new family, but it is better to keep in touch with both your parents.

▲ Talking to a teacher or a friend can help you to adjust if your parents divorce or separate.

Stepfamilies

A stepfamily is created when a parent takes their children into a new relationship or marriage. Some stepfamilies only meet at weekends or during school holidays, while others are full time. Two and a half million children in the UK are growing up in stepfamilies.

While all families are complicated, stepfamilies do present some special challenges, especially at the beginning. Understanding why problems occur can help.

The new stepfamily

For many young people, becoming part of a new stepfamily is not something they look forward to or enjoy. This is not really surprising.

A stepfamily is often created after something particularly painful has happened -- because a parent has died or because of a divorce or permanent separation. Losing a parent in either of these ways is absolutely devastating and can affect you for a long time.

Sandra, aged fourteen, had been living with her mum and her little brother since her dad and mum had divorced two years earlier. She didn't mind her mum having a boyfriend. In fact, she quite liked earning a bit of money babysitting for her brother when they went out. But then one night her mum came in with Barry and announced they were going to get married. They asked Sandra to be their bridesmaid. But Sandra didn't feel a bit excited. In fact, she felt sick. While Barry and her mum celebrated and made plans for their future, Sandra lay crying on her bed.

▲ Many young people dread becoming part of a new step-family, which will change everything for them.

Though Sandra's mum and her boyfriend were full of hope and excitement because they were in love, Sandra was upset. She had just got used to her dad moving out, and now her mum was going to marry someone else. Sandra didn't want to be in a new family. She didn't want a stepdad. She wished her mum and dad could just get back together again.

Parents want their children to be excited about forming a new family. They want them to like their new partner, and they want to make up to their children for the pain they have caused during the divorce. But no one can make up for the loss of a parent. And it is difficult for young people to like someone they hardly know, someone who is making life difficult by changing things.

So, when a parent marries or moves in with someone new, young people often relive the pain they experienced when their parents split up. They are reminded that their parents will never get back together again and they feel that their absent parent is being replaced. This makes them miss that parent all over again, even though the divorce might have happened years ago.

So it is often the case that adults and teenagers go into a step-family with very different feelings.

Step-parents

Fairy tales have given step-parents a reputation for being cruel and murderous. Remember Hansel and Gretel, who were abandoned in the woods by their father at their stepmother's urging? Being a step-parent is one of the hardest jobs in the world. A step-parent is expected to love, feed and clothe children they hardly know and who may hate them.

Although some people get on better with their step-parent than with their real parent, the relationship between a new step-parent and a teenager is usually very strained. They have little or no time to get to know each other before the arguments that are a normal part of adolescence begin. Many young people feel that their step-parent is interfering in their lives. They sometimes try to drive them away by being unkind.

▼ Relationships between you and your step-parent are often more difficult than with your real parent.

Twelve-year-old Darren had lived alone with his dad since his mum had died when he was two. He and his dad were very close and spent a lot of time together going to cricket matches. Every evening they chatted to each other about their day. When his dad's girlfriend, Jasmyn, moved in with them, Darren felt pushed out. While his dad and Jasmyn sat cuddling in the living room, Darren watched television alone in his bedroom. He and his dad no longer discussed the day's events with each other. When Jasmyn started going to cricket matches with them, it was the final straw. Darren blew up at his dad and accused him of loving Jasmyn more than him and not caring about him any more. His dad told him he was selfish and that he should be pleased his dad had found someone to love again.

Darren's dad was so caught up in his love for his girlfriend that he didn't stop to think about how Darren was feeling. He thought Darren should be happy for him, but how could Darren be happy when he felt he was losing his dad? He'd already lost his mum – his dad was all he had left. Luckily, Darren was able to tell his dad how he felt. Eventually his dad understood and apologized. He promised to spend more time alone with Darren. In fact he said he had missed being with him.

◀ **Your parent may not realize what you are going through unless you can explain how you feel.**

▲ **Young people can feel guilty about getting on well with a step-parent, but they do not need to.**

Kamil, aged fifteen, and his stepfather had a lot of arguments but they shared an interest in football and started going to matches together. When Kamil noticed he was beginning to like his stepfather, he felt guilty. He felt he was somehow being disloyal to his real dad. So he started being cold and mean towards his stepfather.

Only children

Young people like Darren who have been the only child in a single-parent family usually have a particularly hard time adapting to having a step-parent. Often these teenagers have had an important role in the household, sharing chores and listening to their parent's problems in the same way that a partner would. Their parent's new relationship can make them feel unwanted.

If you are going through this, tell your parent how you feel. They probably don't realize. Ask them to spend some time alone with you.

Building a new relationship

Gradually, a stepfamily begins to adopt new rules to suit their situation, and the step-parent and stepchildren begin to build their own relationships though this may take years. Sometimes it is difficult to make friends with a step-parent. Of course there is no reason why you should like them, or why they should like you. But you may find that you do, and that you feel bad about it.

Having a good relationship with your step-parent does not harm your relationship with your real parent. Kamil's father would probably have been relieved to hear that they were getting along. Besides, step-parents have a tough time. They need all the friendship they can get. It is miserable to feel unloved by the children you live with.

Changes in your parent

When your parent remarries, you may notice a change in them. A step-parent may bring out aspects of your parent's personality that you have never seen before. This may make you feel like your parent is slipping away from you. But they are just changing in the same way you do when you are with different friends. It is generally nothing to worry about.

▼ Stepbrothers and stepsisters fight just as much as real brothers and sisters.

Stepbrothers and sisters

Andrew was eleven and his sister was ten when their mum remarried. Her new husband and his two sons moved in with them. When Andrew had to share his bedroom with the eldest boy, Hanif, who was sixteen, he wasn't too happy but he tried to accept it. But Hanif started ordering Andrew about, telling him not to touch any of his things. Andrew was furious and tried to grab Hanif's ghetto blaster and throw it out of the room. Hanif told Andrew's mum, who made Andrew stay in for a whole week. Andrew was miserable. He felt his mum had taken Hanif's side against him and that his mum must love Hanif more than him.

Sharing your home and your parent with stepbrothers and sisters is hard to do, especially if one of them takes over your role as the oldest or youngest of the family. Andrew was used to being the oldest. When Hanif came along, Andrew felt he was being pushed out of his place. Andrew's mum was anxious to get along with Hanif, so she tended to be hard on her own son and to take Hanif 's side. Eventually she realized that it wasn't a good idea for Hanif and Andrew to share a room. Once they had their own space, the boys settled down better.

A new baby

When a baby is born into a stepfamily, it can be upsetting for the children who were born before the stepfamily was created. They may feel threatened by the baby and left out, particularly if their parent is so busy with the new child that

▶ It is easy to feel left out when a step-parent takes more notice of a new baby than of you.

they forget to reassure the older children that they still love them. Young people who feel insecure often display their feelings through bad behaviour. If you are feeling uncertain of your parent's love, try to talk to them about it. Let them know that you need their love.

Getting past the crisis

It takes a long time for a stepfamily to get used to each other, sometimes two or three years. During this time some stepfamilies reach a crisis point where all the problems seem too big to solve and no one knows how to make things better. This is a miserable situation to be in. It can even drive some young people away from home. Outside help might be needed to get the stepfamily past this point. The National Stepfamily Association, listed in the back of this book, offers counselling to anyone in a stepfamily.

Friends

Friends are important to everyone, but especially to a teenager. At this time of your life you will be turning more and more to your friends for help and advice. Often you can discuss things with your friends that you might find awkward with an adult – school problems, relationships and sex. When things are bad at home, when you need a shoulder to cry on or someone to talk your problems over with, friends can give you the support you need.

Friends can also make the world a more interesting place. Getting to know people from different backgrounds with different tastes and views will open up your world and help you to form your own opinions.

▶ Everybody needs friends – friends share good times with you and help you out when you're down.

SAB STREET
101 Original designs
LTD.
01 428 6521
FWW 541Y

▲ **Being on the outside at a new school can make you feel very alone.**

Loneliness

Loneliness is a horrible feeling. For some, it is a temporary state. Maybe you have just moved to a new town where you don't know anyone, or maybe your best friend has moved away and you haven't made a new friend yet. If you are in this situation, joining in after-school activities will help you to meet people of your own age with similar interests. For other people, loneliness is a continual problem. They may find it difficult to make friends for a number of reasons.

Shyness

First, there are people who are shy. Everyone feels shy at some time. If you are meeting new people, it is normal to feel self-conscious. You will probably worry about whether you look OK and about what people think of you. You may have physical symptoms of your shyness: sweaty palms, blushing, stammering, or a rapid heartbeat. For some people, these feelings are so strong that they avoid social contact.

There is nothing wrong with being shy, but if it is making you unhappy and preventing you from making friends, there are things you can do. Try to build your confidence by being positive about yourself. Think about all your good points. If you don't know what they are, think about the things you have done that have made other people happy. Then, next time you meet someone, take a deep breath and start up a conversation. You don't have to make a speech. Just ask them where they got their T-shirt or make a comment about what they are doing. Concentrate on making them feel happy and at ease, then you will forget to think about yourself and what they think of you.

Being unpopular

Secondly, there are people who are just unpopular. Maybe you do not fit in for some reason and are bullied or teased. If this is the case, you probably do not like yourself and think you are unattractive or a failure. This makes it hard for you to believe that anyone will like you. Instead of smiling and attracting people to you, you probably hang your head and avoid eye contact or glare at people to keep them away. Think about this as you walk around. Of course it is impossible to grin like a Cheshire cat when you feel miserable, but maybe you can do something to make yourself feel better. If a problem at home is making you miserable, talk to someone about it – maybe a favourite teacher. Regular vigorous exercise will raise your spirits and make you look and feel lively and attractive.

▼ Try to start up conversations with other people.

Keeping friends

There are some people who cannot keep friends because they are unreliable or ask too much of them. If you have trouble keeping friends, think about how each friendship broke up to see if there is a pattern. If you find that in each case you had broken a promise or let out a secret, then you know what went wrong. Don't be too hard on yourself about it. Everyone makes mistakes. Next time you will be more careful.

Bullying

Bullies can make life hell. If you have ever suffered at the hands of a bully, you will know that feeling of dread you get whenever you see one. Some bullies use their strength to frighten people, and others use words.

Understanding why a bully picks on people will help you to get out of their clutches. Bullies pick on people who are physically weaker than they are or easily frightened.

Usually a bully is a very unhappy, frightened person, who feels angry and bitter. Sometimes their behaviour is due to a problem at home, such as their parents going through a divorce. But often their bullying behaviour is an imitation of the way they have been treated by their parents at home.

Bullies tend to pick their victims carefully. Sometimes the victim is a weaker child who is also abused at home and is therefore used to being treated that way without complaining. Another type is a child who is loved at home and completely bewildered by the bully's tactics. In this case the bully is showing envy of children who are loved more than they are. Then there are victims who are 'different' for some reason, maybe because of their size, or race, or because they are new to the school.

◀ Bullies usually pick on someone weaker than they are.

▶ Friends can teach you new skills.

If you are being bullied, try to understand that the bully is probably behaving this way because he or she is jealous or frightened. Tell someone at home or at school what is happening.

If you think that you are a bully, don't despair. Recognizing that you are behaving this way is a good first step to changing your behaviour. You may need help to do this. If you have problems at home, it is important that you get help for your family. Try to talk to a friendly teacher or relative, or to a counsellor if your school has one.

Groups and gangs

It can be wonderful to feel part of a group of people who have fun together. You probably have a lot in common, and being with them makes you feel secure, liked, needed and confident. You can identify with the group. Because these friends are important and you want them to continue to like you, you can easily be influenced by them. They might influence how you wear your hair, your style of clothes and your taste in music. Sometimes friends encourage you to do something that is good fun that you might not have been able to do by yourself, like going to see a band or learning to skateboard.

Though groups can be a positive influence, sometimes they can push you into doing something you do not want to do or that could get you into trouble. You may feel that if you do not do what they want, then they won't be your friends any more.

This is a difficult situation that everyone finds themself in sooner or later, and only you can decide what to do. True friends will like you for yourself, regardless of your decision. The same goes for people who make fun of your interests, for example if you are a boy who wants to be a ballet dancer. If you have the strength to know your own mind and make your own decisions regardless of what people think, everyone will respect you in the long run.

Some groups of young people get involved in serious illegal activity like drug dealing. The pressure to join in can be immense. A life of crime can seem glamorous, but getting involved in something like this will make your life very miserable. Drug dealers usually end up as down-and-out addicts or even dead. They and other young criminals can find themselves wasting their whole youth in prison.

▼ Sometimes friends can push you into doing things you do not want to do.

Romantic relationships

At some point during your teenage years you will probably start to have romantic relationships. These can provide hours of excitement but also hours of torment, wondering whether someone likes you, how to ask them out, and how to deal with rejection if things don't work out.

Crushes

Your first romantic experience may be a crush. A crush, or infatuation, is an obsession with romantic thoughts about someone. Often this person is someone that you are very unlikely to go out with, for example a pop star or a teacher. They may be the same sex as you.

For teenagers, an infatuation is a way of learning to deal with the feeling of love without the complication of a real relationship.

'Am I gay?'

Most people wonder at some point in their life whether they are gay. Sexuality is not a clear-cut issue, with everybody neatly categorized as gay or straight. Some people find they are attracted to both sexes. And it is quite common for young people to experience a period of sexual attraction to the same sex, yet to have heterosexual relationships later on.

▲ Most people dream of having a romantic relationship, but it is not always easy to find the right one.

However, there are some young people who know from an early age that they are homosexual. If you are a homosexual teenager, you will probably find it difficult to be open about your feelings. It is very important to talk to someone freely. If you don't, you will feel isolated and may become depressed. Gay youth groups help homosexual young people meet so that they can share their feelings and experiences. The Gay Switchboard, listed at the end of this book, can put you in touch with a group in your area.

'How do I know if someone likes me?'

You can usually tell if someone likes you by the way they react to you. If they smile when you smile at them and they seem interested in you, then they probably like you. However, this doesn't necessarily mean they want to go out with you. They may not be ready for that kind of relationship, they may have a girlfriend or boyfriend already, or they may be interested in you just as a friend.

The best way of discovering more about them is to make friends and see how things go. This gives you a chance to get to know each other better before you decide whether or not to get involved.

Making friends

You can make friends with the opposite sex in just the same way as with the same sex. If you find it hard to make opposite-sex friends, it may be because you are not used to them. For example, if you are a girl with no brothers, then you might think of boys as an alien species. You probably don't know what kind of things they are interested in or what to talk to them about. If you have this problem, try to find out what their interests are, for example what music they like, their favourite sports, in the same way you would with someone of the same sex. You will find you have something to talk about with most of them.

Asking someone out

It is nerve-racking asking someone out for the first time. There is no right way of doing it. How you set about it will depend on you and the person you are interested in. Probably the easiest

◀ **Try to find out what somebody is interested in, so that you have something to talk about.**

way is to be fairly casual about it. You could start by asking them out as part of a group. For example, you could say, 'We're all going to the fair on Friday night. Do you want to come?' That way it is easy for them to say no without making you feel rejected.

Phoning someone up to ask them out is easier than doing it face to face. It is a good idea to arrange to do something on your first date, like going to the cinema, because during the date you might feel shy and not know what to say, particularly if you don't know the person well. If you go to see a film together, then at least you will have something to talk about.

If the person turns down your offer, you will probably feel embarrassed for a while, but don't let this stop you asking someone else out when you are ready.

First dates

Everyone feels nervous about their first date, worrying what to wear and what to say. It is important to be yourself. Wearing something you feel comfortable in will help you feel more at home. Don't try to project a different personality. For example, don't dress up glamorously if you don't feel happy that way. It is important that your friend sees and likes the real you.

Don't worry if you find you don't like each other that much, and don't feel obliged to go out again if you know it is not what you want. You haven't wasted your time, because each experience of going out teaches you more about what you want and the kind of person you get on with.

'Am I in love?'

Love is a word we use to describe our feelings about our favourite food, our pet, a piece of music, our parents, our boyfriends and girlfriends. But our feelings for

each of these are different. Yet what we feel we have for all of them is a special fondness.

Being 'in love' is different. When you are in love, the world seems like a wonderful place. You feel full of energy and happiness, yet dreamy at the same time. You might feel literally starry-eyed. You and your boyfriend or girlfriend are so strongly attracted to each other you can hardly take your eyes off one another. You feel you have met your soulmate. You like each other so much, you could talk forever.

Though these feelings are beautiful and should be relished, they cannot last at this intensity. Eventually you will take your feelings for granted. Although this is sad in some ways, it would be impossible to carry on with the rest of your life – schoolwork, friends and other interests – if you were continually in this state.

▲ Even if you are nervous on a first date, try to project your own personality.

If you still love each other deeply even after this phase is over, then you have the basis for an excellent and long-lasting relationship.

Breaking up

If things don't work out in a relationship, then someone has to finish it.

Ben had been going out with Sarah for two months. She was really pretty and he liked being seen with her, but she was a bit boring.

Ben didn't know how to tell her, so he stopped showing any interest in her. Every time Sarah phoned, he got his brother to tell her he was out. Sarah didn't know what was going on. She thought Ben must have another girlfriend.

▲ **If you want to finish with somebody, it is better to explain honestly, even if it is difficult.**

Finishing with someone is hard. Many adults have difficulty doing this. It takes courage to tell someone that you no longer feel the same for them. If you want to end a relationship, save yourself and your friend hours of worry by telling them directly. It may seem easier just never to phone them again or not to turn up to the next date, but the mature thing to do is to tell someone straight. Try to keep in mind that you should treat your boyfriend or girlfriend the way you would like to be treated in the same circumstances.

If you are the one who is left with a broken heart, you will probably feel hurt, angry, frightened and lonely. It is horrible to feel rejected by someone you love, but it does not mean you are worthless. You were just not right for each other.

It will probably take you a while to get over the break-up and to feel ready to go out with someone else. In the meantime, staying busy and going out with your other friends will help a lot. Try to talk about your feelings to them. You will feel better before long.

How far to go

Most young people – boys and girls – worry about how far they should go in a relationship. This ranges from worrying about whether it is OK to kiss someone to whether it is OK to have sex. Generally speaking, if you are both happy about it, it is all right, though it is important to know that it is illegal for a boy or man to have sex with a girl who is under 16.

If either of you feels doubtful about something, don't do it – you probably won't enjoy it. You can usually tell how the other person feels by the way they respond. If they seem to be holding back, then they probably want you to stop. Never push someone further than they want to go.

Don't let what other people say or do influence you. If everybody you know says they are having sex, this does not mean that it is true or that you should. Trust your feelings, and wait till you feel it is right for you.

Shona was fourteen. Her boyfriend had been asking her to have sex with him. She didn't want to because she didn't feel that way about him. But when her friends started talking about their sexual experiences, she felt very left out and embarrassed at being a virgin. One night, she told her boyfriend she wanted to have sex with him, even though she didn't really. They were both nervous. They kept their clothes on and didn't even kiss much. It was horrible for both of them – more like a biological experiment at school than making love. The next day Shona felt pretty awful, but she casually told her friends she had lost her virginity. Instead of congratulations, there was a long uncomfortable silence. Shona felt worse when she realised that they had all been lying.

Abusive relationships

Becoming an independent adult and forming new relationships can be exciting and challenging. But you will face difficulties, too. Some people are abusive in their relationships. They treat people in a way that hurts them physically, sexually or psychologically.

Physical abuse

People who physically abuse their partners or children by hitting them are often full of remorse afterwards and promise it will never happen again. But it will. They need help to stop. They may have suffered the same treatment themselves as a child and be incapable of changing alone.

If your parent, boyfriend, girlfriend, or anyone else physically harms you, you must do something about it. Don't believe them if they tell you that you asked for it. Nothing you can say or do justifies physical violence. Tell someone you trust what is going on, or get help from Childline, listed at the end of this book.

▼ If arguments with someone lead to physical abuse, make sure you tell somebody.

▲ **Even in daytime, it is not a good idea to wait on your own in quiet places.**

Indecent assault

Indecent assault occurs when someone forces sexual contact on another person, for example, if someone kisses you, makes you touch them, or touches your genitals, breasts or bottom when you don't want them to. Boys can be indecently assaulted, too.

Karen, aged fifteen, was standing on the bus when she felt the man behind her push his groin against her bottom. At first she thought she was imagining it. She tried to move away, but the bus was packed. Then she felt a sweaty hand slide up her skirt. She turned around and said very loudly, 'Get your hand off my leg.' The man was so surprised, he quickly got off the bus.

▲ There are trained people to help you if you ever get assaulted.

People often choose teenagers and children for their victims because they think they will be too scared to do anything. If you speak up for yourself, they will be taken by surprise.

Rape

Rape victims are usually women or girls, but boys and men are raped, too. You may think that it can't happen to you because you are a careful, sensible person. Unfortunately, this is simply something we tell ourselves to make us feel safe. Even babies and grandmothers are raped. Hopefully it won't happen to you, but knowing something about it may help you if it does.

Rapists like to terrorize people and humiliate them by forcing them to have sex. They do this out of anger, to feel powerful, or because they find their victim's fear thrilling.

You cannot tell a rapist from looking at him. He can be a policeman, a doctor, your boyfriend, or even your dad. In fact, most victims know the person who raped them. Date rape – raping someone on a date – is the most common form of rape.

Sex is not supposed to be a punishment. It should be enjoyed by both people. Some boys and men say that if they have an erection they must be satisfied, that if they aren't their penis will fall off or be damaged. This is not true. Not having sex cannot harm them. You have the right to say 'No' to anything at any time. It doesn't matter how far you have gone, you can still say 'No'.

Sixteen-year-old Samantha was at home alone with her boyfriend, Darryl. They had been kissing and Darryl was touching Samantha's breasts. He wanted her to have sex with him, but she wasn't sure. Darryl told Samantha that if she really loved him she would do it. Samantha said she just wasn't ready yet. Darryl got angry and said she had led him on. He pinned her down and raped her.

If you are unlucky enough to be raped, you will need help to recover. Tell someone what has happened as soon as possible. If you feel too frightened or embarrassed to tell someone you know, contact a Rape Crisis Centre like the one listed at the end of this book. They are run by people who have been through the same ordeal.

Incest

When a parent or another member of your family sexually assaults you, it is called incest. The most common form of incest is committed by a father or stepfather against his daughter or step-daughter, though mothers sometimes sexually assault their children, too.

In many cases, parents who commit incest were sexually abused themselves as children. They tend to think of their children as their property, to deal with as they wish. Sometimes they force sex on their children because they are unable to form a relationship with another adult.

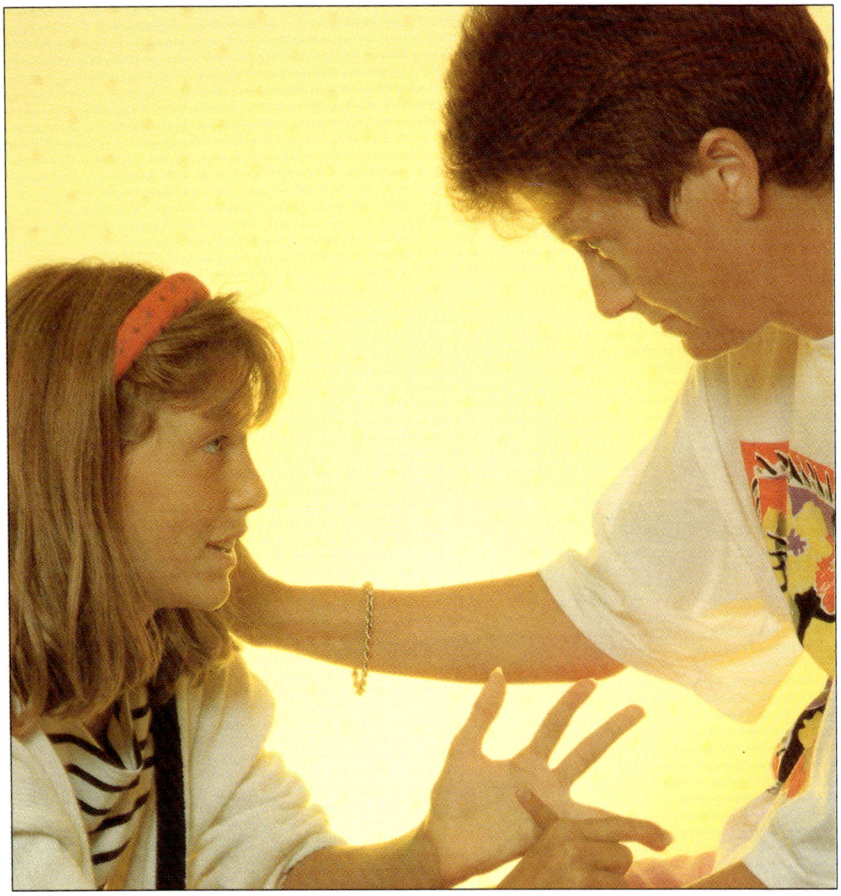

◀ If you are ever assaulted, talk to someone as soon as you can.

▲ If a member of your family sexually assaults you, you will probably need outside help.

◀ **Counsellors will not tell anyone what you have said unless you want them to.**

Being sexually assaulted by a parent is the ultimate betrayal and one of the most awful experiences there is. You have been terrorized by a person who is supposed to protect you. Incest victims usually feel that they are in some way to blame. Maybe they have been told so by the person who assaulted them, but it is definitely not true.

If you are being sexually assaulted by someone in your family, it is vital that these attacks are stopped. You can try to stop them yourself by refusing to take part, but you will probably need outside help. If you cannot talk to a family member, tell a friend or a teacher, or call a professional counsellor. Childline or the Rape Crisis Centre will help you. Their numbers are listed at the end of this book.

Your family will need professional help to sort out this problem.

Usually, counsellors will not tell the police or your parents that you have called unless you ask them to do so. If the police do find out, the person who assaulted you is unlikely to go to prison unless you want them to, as your co-operation would be needed to prosecute them.

Reading about abuse is frightening, but it is important to be aware of what your rights are and why people behave the way they do in case you ever find yourself in an abusive situation. But remember, the majority of people are not abusive or dangerous.

▼ Thankfully, most people are not abusive, threatening or dangerous. It is important not to distrust everyone you meet.

Glossary

absent parent The parent who no longer lives with the family following a divorce or separation.

abuse Treating somebody in a way that hurts them physically, sexually or psychologically.

adolescence The time between being a child and becoming an adult.

ambivalent Having contradictory feelings about a situation, for example, excitement and fear.

delinquent behaviour Doing things that are unacceptable or illegal.

divorce The legal ending of a marriage.

heterosexual Sexually attracted to someone of the opposite sex.

homosexual Sexually attracted to someone of the same sex.

incest A sexual relationship between a child and a member of his or her family. This is against the law.

insecure Lacking in confidence.

rape Having sexual intercourse with someone against his or her will.

separation The situation of a couple who are living apart but not divorced.

siblings Brothers and sisters.

unscrupulous Without a conscience.

Further Reading

Family and Friends
by John Coleman
(Wayland, 1990)

Growing into Sex
by Christine Green
(Wayland, 1989)

Growing Up: A Young Person's Guide to Becoming an Adult
(Merlion, 1993)

Safe, Strong and Streetwise: A Teenage Survival Guide
by Helen Benedict
(Hodder and Stoughton, 1988)

Teenagers Growing Up in a Stepfamily
by Erica De'Ath
(a booklet published by the National Stepfamily Association, 1993)

When Parents Split Up: Divorce Explained to Young People
by Ann Mitchell
(Chambers, 1986)

Useful addresses and phone numbers

Childline
Tel. 0800 1111

Family Planning Information Service
27-35 Mortimer Street
London W1N 7RJ
Tel. 071-636 7866
Or contact your local Family Planning Clinic
or Brook Advisory Centre

Gay Switchboard
Tel. 071-837 7324

The National Stepfamily Association
72 Willesden Lane
London NW6 7TA
Tel. 071-372 0844 (office)
Tel. 071-372 0846 (counselling service)

Rape Crisis Centre
Tel. 071-837 1600

Index